Singled Out or One in the Body?

An Exploration of Singleness in the Church Today

Lakshmi Deshpande

Anglican Chaplain, Nottingham Trent University

GROVE BOOKS LIMITED

RIDLEY HALL RD CAMBRIDGE CB3 9HU

Contents

Acknowledgements

I appreciate everyone who has listened, encouraged, read, commented and contributed to this booklet directly or otherwise, especially Rick and Rachel for their confidence from the start. I hope I have thanked you in person as I continue to thank God for each and all of you.

Dedication

To Emma and Sophie Deshpande, who I pray will always live life fully and will increasingly know and thank the God who gives them hope and joy.

The Cover Illustration is by Peter Ashton

First Impression September 2001
ISSN 0144-171X
ISBN 1 85174 475 4

1
Introduction

[Jesus said] I have come that they might have life and have it to the full
(John 10.10)

Walking into the church alone was hard, especially when everyone else seemed to be with someone in particular. During the notices the minister mentioned the need for Sunday School teachers, delighted in the birth of 'the latest addition to the church family,' talked about the forthcoming marriage enrichment course after reading out the banns of marriage and then commended George to our prayers after the sad loss of his wife. I recalled St Paul's desire that all Christians should be single and wondered about their place in this church...

Reasons for Writing

This booklet arises from a sermon I preached on singleness within the church. Responses to this sermon and my own experience confirmed that many single adults in the church often feel unwittingly ignored or overlooked and thereby not enabled to live fully as members of the body of Christ, either within or outside the church. The experience of church noted above is common to many. Church members and leaders struggle with images of marriage and singleness that lead to the two being polarized. A single church minister was reading the minutes of a meeting he could not attend and came across the phrase 'next time we want a minister with a family.' Examples and illustrations in talks and literature frequently refer to married life, parenthood or living in homes with others.[1]

Perhaps one of the reasons for ignoring issues of singleness in the body of Christ is the lack of clear theology, concerning both single people and what it means to be in the body of Christ in the twenty-first century. Yet about one third[2] of most adult congregations is made up of single people—unmarried, widowed or divorced.[3] So singleness in the church needs to be addressed for practical as well as theological reasons.

Many Christians know what it means to be single in the twenty-first century body of Christ. I hope this booklet will affirm them and help them to see themselves and their experiences in new ways. I hope, too, that married Christians

---

1   I have heard people with disabilities and those from minority ethnic or other groups express similar sentiments about feeling invisible and simply wanting their existence acknowledged.
2   General Synod Board For Social Responsibility, *Something to Celebrate* (London: Church House Publishing, 1995).
3   This does not include married people who for whatever reason are not involved in church with their spouses, so experience church and even being Christian as single people.

will read this so that together, single and married, young and old, we can see ourselves as members of Christ's body with something to offer one another, living life to the full. To begin with we need to define singleness.

The Search for a Positive Description

A single person is one who is not in an exclusive and committed emotional, physical and sexual relationship with another person. If someone has a sexual partner, and the relationship is exclusive with some degree of commitment, then that person is not single. Nor is an individual single who is 'going out with' or engaged to another. If a Christian is in sexual relationships where there is no emotional or other commitment then that seems to be abusive of all parties concerned.

Compared with singleness, marriage is easier to define. A married person has a husband or wife, regardless of the state of happiness of the marriage. But singleness is much harder to define simply, other than *the state of a person who is not married, engaged or going out with someone*. It is negative to describe someone as 'not' something, and therefore essential that we in the church recognize that singleness is not 'what marriage isn't,' nor are single people 'those who have not yet married.' We are then in a position to see that singleness encompasses a range of experiences.

Six 'Ds' of Singleness[4]

The 'Ds' of singleness are useful when exploring the complexity of singleness. People are single for a variety of reasons that can be loosely divided into two groups. The first group of 'Ds' relates to aspects of bereavement. The *death* of a partner leaves the survivor a widow or widower. Similarly *divorce* results in singleness. *Desertion* by a partner might be a precursor to divorce, but the outcome is still that the person is single.

The second group of 'Ds' describes reasons for singleness that are not obviously linked to the loss of someone else. In Matthew's gospel Jesus is questioned about issues of marriage and divorce and responds, 'Some are eunuchs because they were born that way; others were made that way by men; and others have renounced marriage because of the kingdom of heaven' (Matt 19.12). Translated into the twenty-first century, some people are single wholly or partly through *desire*, for example, those who enter religious communities or the Roman Catholic priesthood. Many Christians in these contexts and many others speak of a sense of vocation, God calling them to embrace singleness. There is no sense of such Christians being 'unfortunates.'

On the other hand there are people who would say they were single mostly by *design*—perhaps those in Jesus' statement who were 'born eunuchs' or 'made

---

4   Based on work by the Rev'ds Cedric Blakey and Chris Dyer in Derby.

that way by men.' This might relate to physical, mental or emotional realms. Some Christians speak of themselves as being born gay and hence choose singleness by design rather than desire or calling.[5]

Finally, many Christians are single largely through *default*, which can underlie or be a feature alongside other reasons for singleness. The widower whose wife died in childbirth has not chosen his state, any more than some people that have never married and long for a husband or wife, but have not met a suitable marriage partner.

For an individual there might be one 'D' that is more apparent than others, but there is rarely only one reason for singleness. A nun or monk might be single mainly through desire and design, whilst the single parent who has never been married will have a complicated mixture of design, default and other issues contributing to his or her single state. In my own case I would say at the moment I am single largely through default, not having met anyone I have wanted to marry who has wanted to marry me. Perhaps, too, there is an element of design through the combination of ethnicity and ordained ministry; certainly 'ethnic minority woman minister' is not at the top of many lists of 'qualities in a wife.' However, I increasingly desire singleness rather than to be married to just anyone for the sake of being married. Recognizing aspects of life that have arisen through default is important for everyone, single or otherwise. This way we can acknowledge any inherent pain in someone's circumstances and move beyond a framework of pity to see people as they really are.

Generalizations About Gender and Singleness

In the same way that the church needs to be aware of the variety of reasons for singleness, people need to bear in mind that although in Christ there is neither male nor female (Galatians 3.26) women and men are different. Generalizing about gender differences requires recognition of men or women who do not conform to stereotypes. But it is useful to note some features that might affect the way men and women view singleness.

All human beings need freedom and security, and these are often seen as the two ends of a continuum. On the whole men tend towards valuing freedom whilst women often place a higher value on security. This often affects how men and women respond socially, spiritually and sexually in different ways. For example, women frequently work co-operatively whilst many men prefer to work independently. And women are often better at forming and maintaining close friendships than men. It is important to bear in mind that a man's intentions and means of expression in various relationships might differ from a woman's.

Most churches have significantly more adult women than men, so that

---

5   For further reading see Tim Bradshaw, *The Way Forward?* (London: Hodders, 1997); Thomas Schmidt *Straight and Narrow?* (Leicester: IVP, 1994); Michael Vasey, *Strangers and Friends* (London: Hodders, 1995).

numerically there are more single women than single men around. One large church had to face a growing problem of a number of single men in the congregation 'playing the field' and leaving several single women distraught as a result. The church leaders recognized a pattern of the men having a choice of single women to date so forming relationships without commitment. This was exacerbated by the positive associations of the word 'bachelor,' providing images of freedom from responsibility, and the more negative word 'spinster' with associated ideas of being left on the shelf.

Marriage versus Singleness?

It is easy to put marriage and singleness in opposition to each other where there is unspoken pain or a perception of misfortune about either state. A married friend went to a seminar on singleness at a Christian conference. She was horrified to be picked on by single people who wanted to be married themselves and consequently saw my friend as 'the enemy.' This feeling expressed by single people is not restricted to Christian settings, as anyone will know who has read Bridget Jones' descriptions of 'smug marrieds.'[6]

Married Christians, too, can unintentionally make hurtful comments. A married man distressed a single friend, saying he had so hated being single himself that he now tried to avoid issues around singleness. Problems between married and single people can arise when there is jealousy on either side. If someone's current state feels difficult the natural response is to become defensive, assuming other people cannot understand. Married parents often envy the perceived freedom of those who are single. Many unhappy single people long for companionship and sex and have the idea that both would be constantly available if they were married. Feelings of isolation, guilt and pain can be increased when there is talk about God 'calling' someone to a particular marriage or singleness. This in turn can lead to a sense of condemnation, either externally or internally, 'I should be grateful for…but I am not.' If Jesus came to bring life in all its fullness to all people, regardless of their marital status, then all members of the body of Christ need to discover what that means in their setting. What can help is a theological framework.

Questions

1. What are your experiences of singleness in the church? How might language and attitudes become more inclusive of all people?
2. What are the similarities and differences in the circumstances of single people in your church? How do they fit with the various 'Ds'?
3. How many positive descriptions and definitions of singleness can you create?

6   H Fielding, *Bridget Jones's Diary* (London: Picador, 1996) p 39.

2

Theology, History and the Church Today

To the unmarried and to the widows I say, it would be a fine thing if they were to remain like myself; but if they find continence impossible, let them marry; for it is better to marry than to go on being inflamed with passion. (1 Corinthians 7.8–9 Barclay)

The quaint tone to modern ears of this translation of St Paul's words seems to imply that marriage is a last resort for the sexually incontinent! Obviously this is a misreading of the text, but it highlights the importance of examining what the Bible and tradition say about marriage, singleness and how people work out God's purposes in the body of Christ. The challenge to apply these principles is significant, especially considering that independent single people have only been a major feature of western society since the twentieth century. Our great emphasis on the individual means we fail, even in the church, to value interdependent growth and synergy—the idea that together our response is greater than the sum of individual responses. Old Testament references to the people of God and New Testament images of the body of Christ overflow with ideas of synergy and community. But how is this theology to be worked out?

Old Testament History

Christians worship the Trinity, God in community. The overwhelming message of the first two chapters of Genesis is that God created humanity for relationship with God and with one another. In the beginning God created male and female in God's image (Genesis 1.27). Genesis 2 tells of God creating man and woman together for companionship and sex, wholesome and beautiful: 'Both the man and the woman were naked, and they felt no shame' (Genesis 2.25). All of this changed from Genesis 3 onwards, when relationships first with God, next with individuals and then among communities within the whole of creation became poisoned by sin, selfishness and shame. There was now a lack of openness before God, mistrust between husband and wife, betrayal and unfulfilled longing and the abuse of sex within and outside marriage (Genesis 19). Neither marriage nor singleness was ideal and, as is the case today, both could involve excruciating loneliness. Indeed with the concept of betrothal there were few single people other than through bereavement.

While in the Old Testament marriage was the norm, so were extended families in which the single people in society (widows and orphans) were to be given care and support. In theory there was a place for everyone in God's community. But this would never fully be realised and individual frustration and loneliness would be a feature of the human condition as a result of the Fall.

Jesus and the New Testament

The arrival of Jesus marked the beginning of the new creation. Jesus' life, death and resurrection allowed for redemption of all aspects of human relationships tainted by sin, selfishness and shame. It appears that Jesus himself was single in a society where marriage was expected. He lived a fulfilled life with friends of both sexes, married and single. 'Jesus possessed a universal love, but he constructed a community of men and women who were bound by mutual understanding, values and support. Jesus did not form an exclusionary group of the elite, nor one based on superiority...Jesus' friends were quite ordinary people...'[7] He acknowledged his biological family but also asserted 'whoever does the will of my Father in heaven is my brother and sister and mother' (Matthew 12.50). This points to a wider concept of family not restricted to blood ties. He was uncompromising in his teaching about marriage and divorce (Matt 19.1–10; Mark 10.1–12), challenging not marriage itself, but the thoughtless ways it was sometimes entered and ended. Assuming Jesus was single and celibate, he is the best example of someone who remained single for the sake of God's kingdom, yet enjoyed intimate relationships with other members of society.

Throughout the New Testament marriage continued to be the cultural norm. For St Paul and other writers the focus was on Jesus coming again. Relationships within the kingdom of God needed to be pure and holy (Romans 13.8–14). Because the second coming was considered imminent there was little time to be concerned about family life, and hence, unless you were likely to burn with uncontrollable passion, better to be single (1 Corinthians 7). As time went on it became apparent that daily relationships needed attention and the focus shifted again to the norm of marriage, but with all who were in Christ—Jews, Gentiles, slaves, free, male, female, and (I would add) married and single, being equal members before God. The emphasis of the New Testament is fidelity within marriage and chastity outside marriage, but with little detailed instruction on how the Christian community is to work together to maintain these standards. There is little said directly or practically about how an individual's deepest needs are fulfilled in relationship within the body of Christ.

Church History

Sex and relationships have been areas of concern in the church since the earliest times, perhaps reflecting some of the challenges posed especially by Roman and Greek culture. Second to fourth century church doctrines suggested that intercourse was shameful and anyone interested in church leadership, whether priests, monks or consecrated virgins, should be celibate. Theologians such as Augustine of Hippo developed links between sexuality and the Fall of Adam and Eve. 'Society, marriage, and, if not those, certainly sexual intercourse, were

---

7   A W R Sipe, *Celibacy* (Missouri, USA: Triumph Books) p 186.

fundamentally alien to [Augustine's ideas of] the original definition of human-ity.'[8] The legacy today is that in Roman Catholic and Orthodox churches many, if not all, ordained men are expected to be celibate. Within the church there is an often unarticulated fear of the power of sex. This is exacerbated in a society that uses sex in advertising and suggests that sexual intercourse on my/our own terms is not only a basic human right, but a basic human need.

The Protestant Reformation challenged the need for priests to be celibate and celebrated marriage to the extent that Christian leaders were expected to be married. Marriage has become 'the only state of life which has a consistently argued and generally accepted biblical basis...[so that] there is often a real bias in Protestantism against any fully wholesome view of celibacy.'[9] This raises questions about singleness being equated with celibacy and marriage presumably equated with sexual intercourse and how this affects church leadership.

This brief snapshot of church history has not taken in the expansion of over-seas mission, involving many single people, or other significant changes in the Protestant church relevant to singleness over the centuries. However, at differ-ent times in the history of God's people either the call to celibacy or the call to family life has been proposed as the spiritually superior. The diversity of single-ness today has no cultural parallel in Bible times nor in most of the history of the church. We need to be aware of the lack of role models when examining the body of Christ in the twenty-first century.

Twenty-First Century Body of Christ

Many single adult Christians struggle to discover their places in the body of Christ, since so much activity, and hence visibility, seems to depend on being part of a couple with (preferably) or without children. It is easy to forget that the most important feature of the body of Christ is the head, Jesus himself. In Ro-mans 12 Paul focuses on mutual relationships between people brought together by God's grace, rather than through any merit of their own. Each member of the body of Christ is unique and vital. We belong to one another and to Christ, with-out conforming to a particular type, so that the image of the body is less impor-tant than its purpose and function of showing God's glory in the world.

To enable this to happen God has given gifts—*charismata*—to the church. The list of gifts in Romans 12 is concerned with practical living as well as increasing spiritual knowledge. The descriptions of the body and gifts in 1 Corinthians 12–14 emphasize the interdependence of members of the body in order for the body to function properly. Gifts are given to build up the body and allow the human community to do the work of Christ in society, bringing glory to God.

Therefore the way in which we behave towards one another and work to-

---

8   P Brown, *The Body and Society* (London: Faber & Faber, 1990) p 399.
9   David Gillett, Anne Long and Ruth Fowke, *A Place in the Family?* (Grove Pastoral booklet P 6) p 4.

9

gether in the body is vital. With membership comprising old and young, single and married the church can model relationships that are not hindered by differences in gender, age, marital or social status (Galatians 3.26–28). Philip Yancey speaks of the church providing a window to heaven, rather than simply a mirror to the world.[10] The many who form one body in Christ belong to one another, each belonging to all. By contrast Foulkes recounts the experience of a youth leader who was told that because he was single he could stay behind to clear up the sick![11] His church seemed to forget the single person's need to spend time building up a life outside church duties, and the need to work as a team, so that each person could live fully and the body of Christ thrive.

Some people see celibacy and marriage as gifts from God, to be encouraged among the individuals or couples who have the gifts to build up the body. However, the gifts of singleness and celibacy are rarely encouraged by the wider church community and seen as essential to the function of the body of Christ within society. The problems are significant. It is hard to foster intimacy and sexual expression without that intimacy leading to sexual intercourse. Therefore in the church we are tempted to gloss over sexuality as a gift of God to demonstrate femaleness and maleness as expressions of the divine nature outlined in Genesis 1.27, and to forget that Jesus lived a fulfilled life as a man, alongside women and men and children.[12]

God calls people as they are, redeeming all they have been and growing them into who they will become in the body alongside others. Individuals need to recognize their own calling in community and to recognize the calling of the body as a whole. This involves working through the complex legacy of history that has shaped our attitudes towards sexuality, singleness and marriage, and looking afresh at the Bible in context. Then the church can learn how to use the gifts God has given us in God's service. We can help by becoming clearer about the purpose and roles of singleness and celibacy within the body of Christ and the role of the rest of the body in fulfilling this purpose. This requires a clear discernment of God's call.

Questions
1. If marriage is God's ideal pre-fall, why did Jesus not model it?
2. How might the marital status of the minister affect church leadership? How can single people and others together help build up the church?
3. How might celibacy be a gift in the body of Christ? How can singleness be promoted beyond celibacy and marriage beyond sexual intercourse?

---

10 Philip Yancey, *What's So Amazing About Grace?* (Michigan: Zondervan, 1997) p 262.
11 F Foulkes (Ed), *Sane Sex* (NSW Australia: ANZEA, 1993) p 66.
12 Foulkes, *op cit* p 82.

3
Called to be Single?

Celibacy is characterized by complete devotion to God, free from all ambivalences, a living symbol of the universality and meaning of divine love, and complete availability and devotion to the service of humanity.[13]

The subject of God's call on lives is complex. Calling in this context is not so much about a particular vocation or even permanent lifestyle, but being able to respond to God on a daily as well as longer-term basis. A friend of mine put it well: 'The call of God is always the same—to live creatively and to enable life.' Discerning the call is about understanding how best to bring this about—what to hold on to and what to put down, what to accept and what to strive for. For most people it is possible to believe that God might be calling someone to single-ness for a particular time as a positive aspect of life. There are still people who have a sense of vocation to a celibate life within a religious community or to the Roman Catholic or Orthodox priesthood. But is it possible to equate unwanted singleness and celibacy with a gift from God? As Christians we believe God loves us infinitely and wants the very best for us. In our better moments, all of us, single or otherwise, aspire to know God's love fully and serve those around us completely, as the quotation above states. But celibacy seems a high price to pay for this privilege.

The God Who Calls

When considering calling we need to know God and recognize ourselves before God. Most of us are good at trotting out phrases about God loving us unconditionally, but few of us consistently live as though this is true. It is sometimes too scary to act as if God really wants the best for us, and it can be tempting to make plans and provisions for ourselves. Many Christians have the attitude that if they hate something God will call them into that area of life to test, challenge or humble them. Single people and others can avoid personal responsibility by blaming God and using their resentment of 'God's call' as an excuse for not living life fully.

As Christians we know a God who has demonstrated his love for us through Jesus' birth, death and resurrection and the gifts of the Holy Spirit, the Bible and the church, however mixed a blessing the last might seem. In addition we need to remember that the Christian life can be full of paradox. God created us as sexual beings and gave male and female to each other to delight in, thus grow-

---

13   Sipe, *Celibacy* p 37.

11

ing with each other and with God. Yet Jesus was, it appears, single and celibate. It is essential to recognize the God who allows marriage and singleness and gives contexts for sex and celibacy; the God who loves individuals as we are and yet calls us into relationship with one another; the God who knew us from the beginning and rejoices and suffers with us.

God's Call and Our Desires

'We know our heart of hearts by acknowledging who and what we desire. Further self-knowledge is hammered out in relationships. Desire is refined by the truth of our loves and the fulfilment of our duty to others…'[14] The difficulty is that some of our desires stem from deep-seated cravings from the past, due, for example, to lack of touch or affection within the family. Unmet needs can be hard to own and require healing. It is godly to desire intimate human relationships as expressions of our sexuality and full life in community. However, sometimes we fear that God does not and will not meet our needs. Hence we might retreat from intimate friendships ('I don't want/need marriage') or become demanding within them. Often we have an idea of how we want our lives to be—married to a particular person, with or without children, self-sufficient.

Community and Integrity

In order to respond faithfully to a call from God we need to acknowledge our needs and wants and test them out with other people in the body of Christ, knowing that the attitudes and expectations of others significantly affect how we hear and respond to God's call. Everyone needs appropriately close friendships outside the immediate family but single people lack a partner as a primary focus. It is particularly important, therefore, to cultivate friendships that allow honesty and openness to grow with God and other people. Alone it is easy to feel as if I have missed out on someone or something God provided in the past. With close friends I can discover how God uses me and helps me to live wholly as a single person now, regardless of the past or the future.

A man spoke about having to cope alone with practical tasks such as cooking, cleaning and gardening. He missed the intimacy of sharing such domesticity but recognized that he did not have to live with the stresses and strains of relationships, especially experienced by couples living under the same roof. He belonged to a group of men from the church who met to watch films, eat and drink together and discuss issues of life. His need for social contact was met and as he continued to seek to serve God he discovered that for him, most of the time, issues of sexuality and celibacy were 'not a big deal.' He was free to discover how to live fully in community.

However, it is important to remember that it is possible to respond to a call

---

14 Sipe, *Celibacy* p 70.

from God in one area of life in order to suppress or fulfil another. Issues around singleness can feature strongly in such cases. Two unmarried women were called by God to work as mission partners overseas. Both enjoyed their adventures abroad, met huge numbers of people, were greatly blessed and a blessing to others. Both returned home in their fifties, still unmarried and, to outsiders, both leading active and fulfilled lives. However, the inner reality was different. One of the women struggled with life away from the mission field, eventually realizing her need for activity and leadership stemmed from feeling she had to prove herself to demanding parents. She was desperate to be married, perhaps seeking the love and intimacy she lacked as a child, and she became increasingly bitter about her singleness and childlessness.

The other woman had spent a long time contemplating marriage. She identified where her love of children came from, both positively as a gift from God and out of her own early childhood deprivation. Before working out her call from God as a missionary she fought and then came to terms with a call by God to be single for the foreseeable future. She returned home knowing that her sense of joy and fulfilment overseas was because of rather than in spite of her singleness, and she maintained this attitude of living freely in her call to 'singleness for now.' This woman had integrated the various calls of God on her life, whilst the other woman had been unable to do so and remained driven rather than at peace. Coming to a place of acceptance requires honesty with self, God and close friends with whom the single person can share hopes and fears. It is not easy.

Recognizing God's Call

Sometimes it is possible to recognize a call from God to singleness even after divorce or the death of a partner, especially with the view that 'celibacy is not…meaningless sacrifice, but a celebration of life in full awareness of what [cannot] be because of love.'[15] Love here is for God and the life Jesus brings. A man who had married in his early twenties realized after his divorce that he had never really been single until this point. Since he was convinced that Jesus' promise of fullness of life was for all Christians he worked hard to discover how he could be thankful in his circumstances and live and serve God with integrity. He explored a variety of Christian traditions, which sometimes brought him into conflict with certain church authorities, but also opened up to him the possibility of being whole without a partner. Similarly, the woman whose husband died leaving her with a young child spoke of wanting to be whole as she was for now. This woman's experience was of God calling her to live within a loving church community where she could mourn her husband's death, find support with her child and learn to be single and positive rather than a pitied widow. The atti-

---

15 Sipe, *Celibacy* p 44 .

tudes of these people were that God would equip them for all they faced and that singleness for the present was as much a calling as marriage had been.

Retrospective Calling

It is often easier to see God's provision for our lives as we look back. In an interview a Christian celebrity in his sixties was asked if he ever wanted to be married. He replied that as a younger man he was desperate to marry, partly because he felt as if he was missing out on the companionship and family life he saw his contemporaries enjoying, significantly because he wanted to have sex with a partner and occasionally because people he knew and trusted said they were sure God was calling him to marriage. However, in later life he could see why God had not called him to marry and he now felt called to be single. He had the sense to add that this calling would not be confirmed until he died.

The celebrity could acknowledge God's call as he looked back over his life and recognize God's work in and through him. One single woman recognized her gifts in relating at depth to a wide range of people over long periods of time, in ways that are virtually impossible if not single. She reluctantly came to realize that this could be part of her calling by God to a single life and continued to struggle with the tension between God's provision for wholeness and her own unmet hopes and desires.

However, there are occasions when God is powerfully at work as a result of someone's singleness, but it is hard to equate this to a calling to singleness. Gladys Staines is a striking example. Her husband Graham was a medical missionary in India. Graham and two of their children were brutally murdered by religious extremists and the next day Gladys was interviewed by the press. She spoke of her intense sadness but also of forgiveness, because the Christian God forgives. Her statement was broadcast across India and caused many people who were not Christians to ask for Bibles. They wanted to learn about this powerful God who could inspire a woman whose husband and children had been so cruelly killed not to be bitter.

This terrible bereavement was a catalyst for many people recognizing Jesus and becoming Christians, but I cannot say that God actively called Gladys to be a widow and childless. It is clear only that God did not prevent the tragedy and that some good came out of it. There are parallels with the story in John's gospel, in which Jesus' disciples ask who sinned that a man should be born blind. Jesus replies that neither the man nor his parents sinned, but that this had happened that the work of God might be displayed (John 9.1–3).

The subject of God calling is difficult and finding God in and through unwanted singleness, however this is experienced, is not easy. If others seem to recognize God at work when we cannot, the experience can heighten in us a sense of isolation, bitterness, failure or hopelessness. If divorce, desertion or death are involved there can be feelings of condemnation both internally and expressed by others. Dealing with some of the pain around singleness is the area to which we now turn.

Questions
1. How does your church encourage people to respond to God's call in community? How does this include God calling people to singleness for now?
2. How can your church encourage all members, single or otherwise, to express intimacy and sexuality in godly and life-giving ways to build up the body of Christ?

4
Struggles and Sources of Pain

'You cannot escape from yourself; for God has singled you out. If you refuse to be alone you are rejecting Christ's call to you...' [16]

When asked about the most difficult or painful aspects of being single most people refer to unmet physical, social and sexual needs leading to a sense of loneliness. This is a universal experience, common to individuals before, during and after marriage, on our own or in company. Bonhoeffer speaks positively of being alone. But when we are *lonely* we are unable to recognize the privilege and responsibility of having been singled out by God. Instead we are left with a chasm of emptiness inside. Those who are single can often have this feeling exacerbated because of the attitudes of other people. Human beings are designed to need interaction with others physically, socially, sexually and spiritually so that lack of appropriate company can trigger loneliness. The experience of some single people in church is that one or more of these basic needs is not only unseen by others but actually made harder to bear. Not having one significant other, the single person needs help from the community of the church to grow in freedom and maturity in all areas to live life fully. The church that does not acknowledge the specific challenges to wholeness for its single members condemns itself to unnecessary pain.

Physical Matters
Some churches appear to be oblivious to or terrified of people's physical needs. Touch is often lacking and a single person can become so unused to being touched that he or she becomes fearful or desperate. There are a number of tragic stories of older widowed people who have not had physical contact with another person for days or weeks. Sharing a sign of peace with other people in church with a warm handshake, a hug or a kiss is a start, but few can survive on this as their sole experience of human touch. It can be hard work and not always appropriate constantly to be initiating touch, asking for or simply offering a hug or sticking out a hand, waiting for the other person to shake it. There can be a fear that single men are a danger to children, or single men around children in church can themselves become anxious about other people's responses, so that they feel unable to express affection and parenting gifts. Eventually for some people physical contact can cease to be a natural part of existence; they become suspicious of or paralysed by spontaneous displays of affection and friendship.

---

16   Dietrich Bonhoeffer, *Life Together* (London: SCM Press, 1992) p 57.

Social Matters

Many single people struggle within churches, feeling socially isolated and misunderstood or even patronized. Women who use the title 'Miss' are assumed to be less than twenty-five or over seventy; those who use 'Ms' are 'feminists' (used pejoratively). Single men who can cook and otherwise look after themselves fairly well can be seen as rather odd or perhaps gay (pejoratively).

Social activity can be hard work. Often single people feel they initiate everything socially. Some retreat into working long hours, not taking proper time off and bringing work home as something to do. Single people are occasionally not invited to dinner parties, either because they ruin the numbers or because it is felt that they might feel awkward among so many married couples. Some singles struggle with attending or leaving social events alone, having no one with whom to share the anticipation or the aftermath, regardless of the event itself.

Many single people find holiday periods difficult. Travelling alone there are practical issues about personal safety, paying single room supplements and simply making all the arrangements alone. It can be extremely difficult to find other people with whom to spend a holiday, since those who are willing are not always free at the same time. Practical service such as helping on holiday camps or in shelters for the homeless can use up the time, but such activities are not necessarily restful and refreshing. Sometimes there is a longing for someone close with whom to share a special moment. Christmas can be particularly hard when our own desires come into conflict with the expectations of others. A woman in her forties felt patronized by the question, 'Are you going home for Christmas?' and replied, 'No, I am going to my mother's.'

It is also hard for the single person to discover how to employ time, money and 'who I am' with the lack of a primary focus and intimate relationships of marriage and family. To what extent should I invest in godchildren, nieces, other family, friends, church community? Discovering who, after God, wants or should have first call on my time and energy is not easy for the single person with no dependants.

Sexual Matters

In spite of the stated view of many Christians that sexuality is a gift from God, the church struggles with this area. A number of single people in the church feel that sex and sexuality are personal problems rather than gifts. Often, even when an individual is comfortable with his or her sexuality, others seem unable to cope, so that the single person's sexual desires are forgotten, ignored, misinterpreted or scrutinized. In many churches there is the (not always) unspoken opinion: 'If you are not dead from the waist down you should be!'

Some couples in churches fear intimate friendship with a single person. A widow was deeply hurt after the death of her husband that a particular couple stopped inviting her round for meals. Someone eventually explained that the wife was afraid that the widow, now single and 'available,' would be attracted to her husband. Boundaries are essential for good and satisfying relationships, but these cannot be imposed or maintained solely by one party and need to be negotiated with mutual trust.

If a single person has few friends of the opposite sex there might be a pejorative assumption that he or she is gay or to be pitied for missing out on sexual (not necessarily genital) encounters. On the other hand single people who have a number of friends of the opposite sex are equally condemned for being flirtatious or fussy. ('He was such a nice man.' 'Do you believe they were really "just friends"?' 'When will she settle down?').

The term 'sexuality' in this context refers to God-given maleness or femaleness, recognizing the minority for whom this is unclear biologically. (I make no assumptions here about sexual attraction to the same gender, opposite gender or both.) Within the overall term there are different aspects of sexuality. Affective sexuality is concerned with intimacy, friendship and emotional and psychological expressions of maleness and femaleness. Corporeal sexuality has to do with dress, sensuousness, touch and other aspects of the body. And genital sexuality has to do with physical acts. These features are woven together with biological aspects of being male or female to create a complex whole. The single Christian is limited in expression of genital sexuality and requires the support of the church to express any aspect of individual sexuality appropriately. Meanwhile, every individual needs a number of other people around to grow in wholeness including in his or her sexuality.

Within a society that simultaneously idolizes and trivializes sex the single Christian's lonely road of sexual celibacy is exacerbated when the church ignores, denies or condemns genital sexual urges. Celibacy cannot be achieved by a cookbook formula or by some slick slogan of self-denial, like 'Just say no.'[17] Masturbation can be a difficult subject, especially for single people. Anne Long outlines two possible attitudes to it. In the first, it provides quick relief to sexual energy and in the second it is accompanied by fantasy. She highlights the importance of living in reality, suggesting: 'If masturbation becomes a substitute for real, growing relationships, it is likely to heighten loneliness and longing.'[18] Her advice is to channel energy into real relationships and where possible to offer God unwanted or feared genital drives.

Sadly, many churches view sexuality only in genital terms or leading to genital expression that is forbidden for the single person. What would be more helpful would be to have all aspects of sexuality openly discussed, not simply forbidden and feared. Sipe's approach to the role of the church in addressing this is helpful: 'In spite of the deeply personal aspects of sex, no one should have

---

17 Sipe, *Celibacy* p 190.
18 Gillett *et al*, *A Place in the Family?* p 15.

to be isolated in the search for sexual knowledge and integration. Nor should we be restricted to commercial, exploitative or secret sources for our education and development. We should know all we can about human sexuality, starting with ourselves.'[19]

Condemnation from the Church

In addition to the lack of understanding in many churches about singleness and humanity, some single people feel actively condemned within their churches. One divorced person felt like an outcast: 'I can see why and how my marriage went wrong. I can understand the view of the church that says I can never re-marry. What I cannot accept is that as a Christian who is divorced I am to live in condemnation by the church for ever.' Christians who are gay often feel unable to acknowledge their sexual orientation and sense it is futile to seek support within the church to live fully and appropriately. Many churches struggle to help divorced or gay or other single Christians to develop appropriate friend-ships and other relationships within the body of Christ, and appear simply to challenge any relationship that appears to be romantic.

Mothering Sunday and other services with a seeming child or (nuclear) fam-ily focus can either ignore single people or unwittingly fall into pitying or pa-tronizing them. Sometimes what is said from the front is appropriate, but the single people sitting on their own can feel excluded, whether or not they con-tribute to their own exclusion. Church advertisements, events, examples in ser-mons or anything else that regularly focuses on couples or nuclear families without mentioning single people or providing integrated alternatives for them condemns the single people in the body.

Issues of Loss

Unfulfilled hopes can be sources of acute sorrow. Barbara Morley writes a moving account of her pain in not being able to be a mother because she is single.[20] Many people have deep, realistic but ultimately unrealized hopes. The sight of an older couple holding hands can bring tears to the eyes of the divorcee who had hoped for lifelong marriage and to the widower who had hoped to share retirement with his wife. Catching a glimpse of young newly-weds might bring a stab of pain to the gay Christian who had hoped for life to be different or the unmarried forty-year-old who had hoped to marry before the age of thirty— the list is endless.

Many single people condemn themselves rather than live with loss. Losing a partner through death, divorce or other misfortune often leads to self-recrimination. People who have never married might blame their appearance,

19 Sipe, *Celibacy* p 28.
20 B Morley, 'Grieving for what has never been' in *Contact: The Interdisciplinary Journal of Pastoral Studies*, No 120, Leicester, 1996.

personality, family or circumstances for remaining single. Such feelings can lead to bitterness and a destructive desire to shut out other people and God.

A Way Forward

The story of Ruth in the Bible is full of pain and hope. In the first chapter Naomi, widowed and childless, asks no longer to be called Naomi, but Mara, meaning 'bitter' (1.20). However, it is as she expresses her bitterness and pain within the community of God's people that her life is transformed and her hopes unexpectedly fulfilled by God (4.14–17). If we spend time being open, honest and alone with God the real sources of pain can be unearthed and grieved. Then singleness can become not the reason for the pain but its context.

Putting hopes to death before God is unbelievably painful and liberating. It was after I had crucified the hope of being a biological mother that I was free to love the children around me without an empty longing inside. The cross involves choosing reality over appearances, integrity and honesty over the temptation to settle for a fantasy. One of the paradoxes of being a Christian is that the more fully we live, the more life we need to let go. Yet as we experience pain, anger and bitterness in God's presence we are able to confess our wrong thinking and actions and receive healing and forgiveness. This is a process that requires trust among Christians and is never easy. But eventually anger and bitterness are replaced by genuine thankfulness. The ache subsides and might return, but never so sharply. The wound might always be there, but Jesus showed his wounds to the disciples after his resurrection, not as sources of pain but of joy and real hope. The hallmarks of Christianity are love, suffering, sacrifice and forgiveness. As together we bring our sources of condemnation to the cross they can be transformed and we can choose to live more fully as members of the body of Christ.

Questions

1. How can churches address with compassion and integrity the challenge that Christian morality makes life more difficult for single people within the church than those outside?[21]
2. What is the place of repentance for the wider church community, and for single people within the church community, when considering aspects of loss and condemnation? How might this happen practically?

---

21 Some church members see nothing wrong with sexual intercourse before marriage. That is not the view here due to integrity of sexuality and personhood.

5

Towards Individual and Corporate Integrity

'Sex is not easy to understand. Celibacy is not easy to understand; perhaps that is why serious discussions of the course of celibate/sexual integration are not more frequent. Also, celibacy is counter-cultural…But commitment to the process does have boldness and genius and power in it.'[22]

The people who live most freely are those who are most integrated, who recognize life as it really is and live with reality rather than in fantasy. Jesus himself said that listening to him, the most real person ever to exist, 'you will know the truth and the truth will set you free' (John 8.32). Every integrated person acknowledges true hope, but lives in the moment rather than the past or the future. So, to live fully and freely an individual requires significant celibate/sexual integration. Single people also need to recognize the issues around living in the counter-cultural way suggested above, since within and outside the church singleness is not the norm.

God always provides choices for a Christian, however difficult it might be to recognize or to live out these choices. That said, the choices for single people are often different from those of others who are not single. Of course there are people who will say or feel they had no choice about getting married; that they were forced into it by friends, family or circumstances. Yet the system with banns of marriage and vows declared in public of 'I will,' signifying a reasoned approach, means that there is choice at different stages to continue or not. Most single people find it hard to recognize an equivalent choice for themselves and need to discover how to live with what they have.

Individual Responsibilities and Choices

When asked about the best aspects of being single many people speak about the diversity of friendships, having time for other people, relative freedom in use of time, money and space, and having privacy. As with any gifts there are inherent difficulties and dangers. Nevertheless, the positive side of being single can be celebrated once the process, explained in the previous section, of acknowledging loss and moving on with Christ has been undertaken.

Jesus said that even he came not to be served but to serve and to give his life as a ransom for many (Mark 10.45). Created, loved and equipped by God we thereby have the freedom and responsibility to love, serve and be served by God and other people. Service needs to come from security, rather than need,

---

[22] Sipe, *Celibacy* p 180.

and this requires depth of relationship with God. In fact, prayer is central to physical, emotional and sexual integration. It is only with God that we can come to the cross and choose not to settle for a sham but to live with reality.[23] There are no shortcuts to living fully. It is only possible by God's grace, as we choose, gradually and perhaps painfully, to let go of cherished hopes and dreams and instead take hold of the best that Christ offers. Jesus was completely aware of who he was and the power and authority God had given him. Because of this, he was able to wash his disciples' feet (John 13.1–17).

Learning to accept by God's grace singleness for the time being without focusing on the future, facing the associated joys and pains, allows deeper service and freedom. It can be hard to discover how to work this out practically. However, the single person is free to serve a wide variety of people when directed and enabled by God. Many single adults enjoy being accepted as members of families within churches, as surrogate siblings, aunts, uncles or grandparents. Several teenagers have benefited from friendships with single adults outside the immediate family who have time to spend with individual youngsters, often in ways that parents might want, but the current stage of relationship with their son or daughter does not allow. The encouragement of other single people can be inspiring to an individual learning to serve.

On a physical level all of us have a responsibility to care for and employ the gifts God has given us in our bodies. Good physical and mental health are gifts, not rights, and need to be sensibly maintained by getting the right balance of food, exercise, rest, work, company and space. Many women and men struggle to integrate body, soul, mind and spirit. Single people especially, although not exclusively, can become fearful of or obsessed with their physical appearance. There can be a feeling, 'If I were somehow different I would not be alone.' It takes time and honesty to learn to be content before God, and those who manage this are often the most attractive. They are suitably careful with their appearance and personal well-being, recognizing the body as a temple of the Holy Spirit, but they are free from vanity or the need to conform to a particular image.

A number of single people cultivate friendships involving significant touch; this is often easier for women than for men, both in same-sex and opposite-sex encounters. Many single people have pets they can stroke so that there is a level of physical care and affection in their lives, albeit not always human. Several women and men enjoy touch through massage, either for their whole bodies or sometimes simply hands, feet or faces.

Corporate Responsibilities and Choices

'A church forum on sexuality involving married people as well as singles can do a lot to eliminate the resentment singles often feel towards the married for

23   Sipe, *Celibacy* p 83.

being insensitive.'[24] This is undoubtedly the case, and there are choices members of the body of Christ can make to incorporate single people more fully. To begin with, the many single people in the body need to be recognized as unique individuals, each with different factors enhancing his or her singleness. Some will be more content in their single state than others, but none will want pity or envy or thoughtless comments. Marriage is not the solution to the 'problem' of the single person, especially if that person does not see himself or herself as a problem. Instead, single or otherwise, people need to learn to be as thankful as possible in their own circumstances, so that they are not afraid of others. As we come to terms with our own hopes and fears we can stay alongside others in theirs as different but equal before God.

In practical terms this means remembering that churches can play a part in helping single people to celebrate significant events, such as birthdays or changes in jobs or home, by planning parties with or for them. Discovering what is important to the single members of congregations as well as including them in the joys of weddings, births and other aspects of family life can enrich the whole body. It might be appropriate for families to invite single friends for holidays or Christmas because of friendship, rather than out of pity or duty. Accompanying single people to and from social events takes away the difficulty of entering or leaving a crowd alone. After a party a single woman invited a few friends to her home for a drink so that she could unwind in close company and did not have to enter her empty house on her own. A number of single men and women value friends who allow them to offer as well as receive hospitality, sharing meals and other aspects of life together. Relationships of trust that are 'unseen' in public can allow single people opportunities to cuddle children and enjoy other intimate aspects of family life.

In addition to social events there are a number of skills and areas of expertise that single and other members of the church can share with one another. Moving house, overhauling a garden, arranging legal, financial and social affairs after the death of a loved one or even shopping, cooking and cleaning when unwell or especially busy can be hard work alone. At such times other members of the body of Christ helping out can be tangible gifts from God. 'Noticing a need and offering help on specific occasions is more valuable than vaguely saying, 'do tell me if there's ever anything I can do.'[25] This booklet has come about because while I was writing Sue and Andy not only offered me the use of their computer, but also fed me, encouraged me and generally anticipated my needs, at the same time allowing me to give to them when appropriate. When flexible boundaries of friendship are established, maintained and re-negotiated between single peo-

---

24 J Duin, *Sex and the Single Christian* (London: Marshall-Pickering, 1990) p 102.
25 Gillett *et al*, p 21.

ple and others together, each and all of us are encouraged to live life fully.

> We do not help Christians who want to practice celibacy if we minimize the difficulty of its achievement. No [single person] can ignore the absolute necessity of facing all of his or her desires if he or she wants to succeed. It is no easy task, since despite help from friends and advisers, each must essentially fight alone in a long, lonely battle...The cost is crucifixion called self-knowledge that involves fearlessly facing all one's desires. One reason why religious celibacy can speak with the voice of moral authority is that it tells the truth about self and human desire...[26]

Is singleness a gift or a handicap? If it is a gift, then the church needs to rejoice in this feature of life, given by God somehow to build up the body of Christ. If singleness is a handicap, because it does not allow the individual to enter the deepest possible relationship with one other person, then that raises interesting questions about Jesus. It also means that the church needs to make provision for the third of most adult congregations that need to learn to live with this handicap in a Christ-like manner. In either case the church at large, as well as single people individually, need to take seriously what it is to be single in the body of Christ and allow God to work in and through each and all of us to God's glory.

Questions
1. What are the individual and corporate stages in accepting singleness for now? Do you see singleness as a gift or a handicap?
2. How can your church help single people and others work towards physical, mental, emotional, sexual and spiritual integration and wholeness? What and how do members of the church celebrate together? What has struck you in particular in reading this booklet? What might you do as a result for yourself and/or within your church?

Suggestions for Further Reading
A Hsu, *The Single Issue*, (Leicester: IVP, 1998)
K Keay, *Letters from a Soul Survivor* (London: Hodders, 1991)

---

26 Sipe, *Celibacy* p 71.